They Call Me Mother Graham

Here is an intimate, loving account reflecting the years that shaped the greatest evangelist of our time—Billy Graham. Morrow Coffey Graham, the remarkable woman who is the mother of "Billy Frank," shares a wealth of family memories, as only a mother can do. In a day when the bonds that hold families together are unraveling as never before, *They Call Me Mother Graham* stands as a striking example of the power that Christ can have in the home. This is family life which develops dynamic personal relationships that Billy and his sisters and brother carry with them to this day.

They Call Me Mother Graham

Morrow C. Graham

Library of Congress Cataloging in Publication Data
Graham, Morrow C.   1892-1981
    They call me Mother Graham.

    Autobiographical.
    1. Graham, Morrow C., 1892-1981   2. Graham,
William Franklin, 1918- 3. Baptist—North Carolina—
Charlotte—Biography. 4. Charlotte, N.C.—Biography.
I. Title.
BX6495.G663A35   269'.2'0924 [B]   77-5617
ISBN 978-1-59328-154-0
Previous ISBN 0-8007-9000-6

CONTENTS

"I was country bred and country raised. My father named me Morrow Coffey." Here is a picture of her holding young Billy Frank. *Below*: "Billy was just a young boy when he walked down that sawdust-covered aisle in response to Mordecai Ham's invitation. This picture of Billy and his father on either side of Mordecai was taken many years after that, in 1953."

"Here we are as a complete family in 1962. Catherine is in back of me, Melvin is next to Billy, and Jean stands behind her father." *Below*: "Billy has always liked this picture."

Chapter One

Our Home

*By wisdom a house is built, and
through understanding it is established.*
Proverbs 24:3, NIV

"Come in, come in, you are so welcome." That's what I'd say if you came to visit in our family home. I'd open wide the door and greet you with much affection. But you can't come, and I'm not having many visitors anymore. Still, the publisher of this book thought that we should have the opportunity to visit together, and so this is being written. It will be a rather one-sided conversation, to be sure, but perhaps I can answer some of the questions that are in your mind as I think back and recall things people have asked me over the years. Yes, I know, the world is interested in knowing as much as possible about my son Billy and the other children.

I had no way of knowing, of course, that Billy Frank (you'll have to get used to hearing me call him that) was going to become so well-known, or I surely would have made notes through those growing-up years, and we would have taken more pictures of him. Today I look at the old pictures in our family album and all I can see are some little faded images.

Billy Frank has two sisters and one brother. Billy is the oldest, followed by Catherine, Melvin and Jean. But that's getting ahead of the story.

The house that I live in is the home that we, as a family, lived in since 1927. I just love every plank and every old nail in it. Our daughter Jean was born here, but the three older children were born in the older place which was just about a block away. That home was torn down and the property sold. We're sorry now that we had the old house taken down; but today where the home originally stood there is a twelve-story office building with a little memorial plaque inscribed:

Birthplace of Dr. Billy Graham
Born November 7, 1918
World Renowned Evangelist, Author, and Educator
Preacher of the Gospel of Christ
to more people than any other man in history.

"Billy Graham is one of the giants of our time. Truly a man of God. The force of his spirit has ennobled millions in this and other lands. I salute him with deep affection and profound respect."

Richard Nixon
President of the United States

This marker dedicated on the fifteenth day
of October, 1971.

My husband, Frank, inherited a 300-acre farm after his parents died. Actually it was all that was left of the Graham family estate after the ravages of the Civil War. He brought me here following our wedding and honeymoon. In those days the house was surrounded by gently rolling fields and pasture land. Today those fields have been taken over by a shopping center. It's quite a different view when I look out the windows now. Where the big barn and two silos once stood is a ten-story office building. There are neon lights at night, casting multicolored patterns over the arbor of muscadine grapes that Billy helped to plant as a boy.

The Book of Psalms says, *"For a thousand years in Your sight are like yesterday when it is past, and like a watch in the night"* (Psalm 90:4).

"... We spend our years as a tale that is told" (Psalm 90:9, KJV). And isn't that true? But we are also told to *"... number our days aright, that we may gain a heart of wisdom"* (Psalm 90:12, NIV).

As long as the Lord spares my life, I plan to retain our family home. The house itself is well-surrounded by large, old trees which Mr. [Frank] Graham himself set out long years ago. At that time it was all country out here. Charlotte was a city of about 35,000. Today it is over 550,000.

The first two years of our marriage we had no running water, electricity, or inside plumbing in our home. There were few other residents on Park Road, perhaps four or five. We did have one neighbor who cooperated with my husband to try and get city lights. I remember so well that the other neighbors said, "No, Frank, it can't be done," and they would have no part of it. But Frank and our good neighbor, Mr. Ashcraft, decided to try and do something for their "women folk" as they called us.

It was a joyous day for me when the old wood stove could go. Mrs. Ashcraft and I were the first two women in the county to have electric ranges. Mr. Graham bought me one of those great big, black Westinghouse electric ranges and I thought it was the grandest thing on earth! We had never seen anything like that, you know.

And then the two men went to work on city water. Again the other neighbors said, "No, it can't be done," but my Frank had a way about him for getting things done, and so did Mr. Ashcraft. In less than a year from the time they started the project we had city water.

Our new home was considered one of the finest in our particular area of Charlotte. It is a large, two-story, red brick home. It is a home that holds many cherished memories. When you come in my front door you are in the living room. I like cool colors and the rooms are painted a blue-green hue with draperies to match. To the left of the front entrance off the living room is the dining room. Off the dining room is the breakfast room, and off from that is the kitchen. In one corner of my kitchen there stands an old-fashioned cupboard which yielded many snacks to the children's eager hands through the years.

As you leave the kitchen you enter a hallway where you would see that I have many bookshelves and books. We were a reading family, but I've given many of my books away. Off this hallway is the downstairs bathroom and my bedroom. This bedroom was formerly our family room, however, and it was here that we gathered nightly for our Bible reading and prayer time together.

If I were giving you a little tour through the house, I'd take you back into the hall, point to the stairs and say that there are four bedrooms up there. But I no longer go up and down the stairs. Then we are right back in the living room where we started. To the right of the hall door as we come out is a massive chest. You would see a large picture of Billy above it, which was done by the famous New York photographer Bachrach. On the chest itself is a favorite photo of my late husband, and nearby, on the wall, a picture of Melvin that I particularly like.

By the front door is a table with an open Bible. You would note that it is a well-worn Bible with many verses underlined.

My house has many items which the children have provided for me and lovely gifts which they, their children, and friends have given to me through the years. There is a fireplace in the living room which provided many a cozy fire for the family to gather around. Near the fireplace are the books Billy has written, all autographed by him with special sentiments for me. Billy has always been so thoughtful.

It is a roomy, rambling house, and was just right for our growing family. Frank had a little office off the living room with a metal desk and a phone. He had always dreamed of having a large dairy herd and it did become a reality. On the wall leading into this office is a picture I am very fond of. Billy gave it to me when he was in Florida. He was nineteen at the time and he wrote on it, "To the dearest Mom in all the world."

Suburban Charlotte gradually spread out, and the milk route Frank established was growing. I was able to assist my husband with cow production records and help with the monthly dispatching of billings. When Melvin and Billy got to the right age, and their father considered them ready, they had to learn to do their share of the farm work.

I've lived here in the farm home on this land for many years. But, you know, it really doesn't matter where we live. Our homes here on earth are only temporary dwelling places.

There is a beautiful secret place of security so wonderfully described in Psalm 91. There we are reminded that

> *He who dwells in the secret place of the Most High shall abide under the shadow of the Almighty. I will say of the Lord, "He is my refuge and my fortress; my God, in Him I will trust."*
>
> Psalm 91:1, 2

And then I like John 14 so well. It speaks of our eternal home in heaven.

> *Let not your heart be troubled; you believe in God, believe also in Me. In My Father's house are many mansions; if it were not so, I would have told you. I go to prepare a place for you. And if I go and prepare a place for you, I will come again and receive you to Myself; that where I am, there you may be also.*
>
> John 14:1–3

It is a wonderful thing to know what your eternal destiny will be. For those of us who know the Lord, that means heaven, to be with the Father and the Son. Mr. Graham went to be there in 1962. One of these days I'll be going there also. Then I will really be at home.

CHAPTER TWO
Those Early Years

A wife of noble character who can find? She is worth far more than rubies. Her husband has full confidence in her and lacks nothing of value. She brings him good, not harm, all the days of her life.

Proverbs 31:10–12, NIV

Those words are very meaningful and beautiful. I read them as a young girl, and I aspired to be that kind of woman.

I have always lived just a few miles from the site of my birth. In a day and age when people move around so much, that's quite unusual, I know. I was born February 23, 1892, right on the farm in Mecklenburg County, North Carolina. I was country-bred and country-raised. I can trace my ancestry to the Scottish pioneers who settled in the Carolinas before the Revolutionary War. One of the signers of the Declaration of Independence, Ezra Alexander, was a relative, as was President James K. Polk.

My father, Ben Coffey, was a Civil War veteran. Early in my life I heard of the horrors of the fighting that raged between the North and the South. The South was still smarting from that, even after I came along. My father was a one-legged, one-eyed Confederate veteran, living proof of the horror of that war. But he was a man with a lot of vim and vigor, and made a better living and worked harder with his one eye and one leg than a lot of men could with two. I thought my father was the smartest, finest, most honest man alive. I knew he was courageous, too. He had a letter from his captain dated August 1863, in which the captain stated: "Benny was such a good boy that I would rather have seen almost any other boy wounded than Benny. There was never cause for reproach, and I never had to reprove him. All the other fellows knew I had a special fondness for Benny."

That letter always thrilled us. I made certain Billy Frank and Melvin read it. The letter went on to explain that my father had been shot in the left leg and lay on the battlefield several hours. While he was waiting to be taken off the field a shell burst nearby, putting out his right eye.

One of the highlights of my life was the time, some years ago, when Billy took me to visit President Eisenhower at Gettysburg, and I was shown the battlefield and the approximate spot where my father had fought and fallen.

I have always felt that Billy's vitality was much like my father's. In physical characteristics Billy resembles my side of the family—blond and blue eyes, strong-jawed and tall—but I am referring more to the drive I saw in my father. Billy has it also.

People have often questioned me about my unusual name. It is an old family name. My father's full name was Benjamin Morrow Coffey, and he wanted his last child to carry that name. Mother was forty-two when I was born. The war had disorganized all home life and Papa knew I would be their last child. He wouldn't allow Mama to give me a middle name. Of course I was supposed to be a son, but when I turned out to be a girl, he wasn't about to change his mind about the name!

As a family we attended the Steele Creek Community Church. It was a large church then, about a thousand members, and it is still a large church today. The zenith of our week was going to church, particularly the Sunday night services. My sisters and I walked the two miles and had the grandest time. We would sing all the way there and then back. As we walked we'd swing our arms and skip along the dusty road.

What did I look like? I had blond, very curly hair, just like an old-fashioned washboard, wavy-curly, hanging way below my waist (that's the way we wore it then).

Mama was a beautiful seamstress. I learned how to sew from her. Her little stitches looked just like machine stitches. She loved pretty things and she passed on to us that appreciation for fine things. My sewing skills later helped supply clothing in lean years to my growing family. I actually did all of our sewing. I made my husband's, Billy Frank's, and Melvin's shirts. I sewed until Jean married, and then I finally gave my machine away.

We read the Bible in our home and had prayers together as a family. My mother and father were looking for the Lord's return, and they instilled in us the fact that Jesus is coming back. We were always faithful at church, both for Sunday services and special functions. It was quite natural, therefore, for me to come into a relationship with Christ. I remember as a young girl going into my room and locking the door and taking the Bible and reading it. I memorized much of the long Psalm 119 and it meant so much to me.

I believe it is even as Scripture says, "*For precept must be upon precept, precept upon precept; line upon line, line upon line; here a little, and there a little*" (Isaiah 28:10, KJV). I gathered a little here and a little there, added from my own study, and after a while it made a whole. All of the teaching and the learning contribute to the making of the whole man or woman. That's why it is so vitally important that we and our children are exposed to good teaching through the years.

I met my husband while attending a house party with one of my close friends. She had some girls up from Atlanta, with five invited guests, myself included. I had previously seen Frank Graham two or three times, but had never been introduced. I wanted to meet him so badly and, in fact, I prayed about it and asked the Lord that if it were in His will, could I please meet that handsome young man! All the girls liked him and wanted to date him, but I felt strongly drawn to him. He was really the answer to a maiden's dream with his black, wavy hair. He was tall and handsome, and walked so straight. But Frank was drawn to me also, and it was in God's will!

He was not only grand looking, but he also had the best-looking horse and buggy in Mecklenburg County. If today's young girls are impressed with the sport cars the fellows drive, we girls were every bit as impressed with Frank's sporty rig and his sleek, fast horse.

Frank asked if he could take me home the night of the party, and of course I said yes. He spirited me away from the park with a flourish that left nothing to be desired.

The horse, its head held high, kicked up its heels, and off we went. My girl friends watched enviously—choking on the dust! I thought I was on a cloud! I walked on air all week after hearing his words, "Morrow, I'd like to see you again Saturday night." I thought Saturday would never come.

Our romance lasted six years before Frank felt he was able to provide for me. It's a good thing he had such a fine horse and buggy, for he made many trips to see me. He took me to church every Sunday night, and we had some nice social affairs there which we never missed. Mr. Graham was good about taking me to musicals in the winter months, and we saw a lot of each other during those waiting years. Frank always dressed well, and I was so proud and happy to be with him. He had an experience with the Lord when he was eighteen and was converted at a revival meeting similar to the kind of meeting where our son Billy Frank would come to his relationship with the Lord.

Mama couldn't afford to give us a big wedding, but it was a happy occasion when we said our marriage vows on October 26, 1916. We had waited so long. Frank said I looked like a fragile doll, with golden colored ringlets cascading around my face. The immediate families and a few close friends were in attendance. Frank whisked me away to Asheville, where we stayed in a hotel for a five-day honeymoon. It was so exciting! We traveled by train.

But soon our five-day honeymoon was over. We left the 250-room Biltmore House and came back to Charlotte and our own country place. I was anxious to make a comfortable, happy home for Frank. Neither of us could know what the Lord was going to bring into our lives, but we were happy in our mutual love for each other, and confident that God would bless our marriage.

Frank was determined at the outset of our marriage that I would not have the demanding job of maintaining a garden. He certainly didn't have the time, "Morrow," he said to me, "it takes too much thought and energy, and you're not a big woman, nor too strong." He was very set in some of his ways, but also very wise.

I did convince Frank to plant cornfield beans and tomatoes. "I've got to have vegetables for canning, Frank," I told him. It was not at all unusual for me to gather two and one-half bushels in an afternoon, and my husband would bring them up later. By eleven o'clock at night I would have them all strung and ready for canning early the next morning. At the end of a busy season, I could count at least five hundred jars of home canned fruits and vegetables. If I didn't have at least that many, I would think I didn't have enough.

It was the year 1918. It was to go down in history as an important year. In November of that year I walked a good half mile down into the cornfield one afternoon. I wrapped my long blond hair around my head in coils of thick braids the way Frank liked it, and spent much of that afternoon picking beans. When I returned to the house, my back ached a little. As I sat in the kitchen, I wondered momentarily if I should have done all that work, but I busied myself stringing the beans.

At one the next morning I awakened my husband. "Frank. Frank," I said to him, "I think you'd better go for the nurse." I was having labor pains.

Seventeen hours later, at five in the afternoon, the baby was born. I looked at my husband and said, "What date is it, Frank?" My husband looked at me tenderly and said, "It's November seventh, Morrow, and we have a fine little son." He weighed seven pounds, seven ounces and was bald-headed. Now the old frame farmhouse would echo with the sounds of little William Franklin, Jr.

Billy Frank sounded like all other newborn babies, but his cries did touch my mother-heart in a special way. In those days you stayed in bed nine days. Why, they didn't even want you to turn over! I look at young mothers today, and how quickly they get them up in the hospital, and how fast they recover, and I am amazed. I was anxious to be up and about taking care of my new little son.

Eighteen months later our next child was born, a girl. We named her Catherine. Catherine cried more than Billy Frank, and I had my hands full. Between baby Catherine and toddler Billy, there were few dull moments. Billy was a climber. When he wasn't climbing, he was reaching or leaping. He scrambled many eggs on the kitchen floor for me, and pulled plates off the table with regularity! Another writer, in describing Billy's toddler days, said that at one moment he was a towheaded angel in disguise, and the next, a not-so-gentle bulldozer knocking over everything in his way. That was literally true!

When Catherine was about a year old she swallowed a safety

pin. This was the first major crisis Mr. Graham and I faced in our married life. The pin lodged near Catherine's heart and they could not operate. The doctors worked on her for five hours, then near dawn we consented to let the doctor push the pin into her stomach. They were finally able to remove it. Baby Catherine was at death's door for six weeks, with the doctors not expecting her to live from one day to the next. My sister was a great comfort and help to me at that time. It was a terrible thing for Mr. Graham and myself, but I clung to my belief that God was going to spare her, and He did. We knew that God brought her through that ordeal in answer to prayer.

In 1924 our second son, Melvin, was born. Billy was six at the time. Those were busy, hard years. Billy's playground was the whole outdoors—and he needed it! Seldom did he walk; he was always running and zooming. I was relieved when he started school.

Billy rode the school bus to Sharon Grammar School. He wasn't the brightest student, but he was one of the biggest for his age. Billy was always tall. I'm afraid Billy Frank learned many things the hard way—like eating his noon lunch at recess and then being hungry the rest of the day. He took some beatings at the hands of the school bully and ended up with black eyes, scraped knees and loose teeth; Billy had long legs and soon learned to use them.

In 1927 Billy Sunday came to Charlotte. Life for us after that was never quite the same. Billy Sunday was everything the newspapers and people said he was. Someone once described him as God's athlete turned preacher, God's acrobat, and God's Gospel showman. He was certainly unconventional. He was a colorful and mighty preacher. My husband took our Billy Frank by the hand and said, "We're going to go hear him."

We were awed by the gigantic frame tabernacle erected for the meetings. There were hundreds of wooden benches, and the dirt aisles were covered with sawdust. Billy Frank was impressed by the fact that Billy Sunday had been a great athlete and a former big league ballplayer. Understandably this would impress a small boy who was himself interested in baseball.

Billy was fascinated by the service. The singing was unlike anything we'd ever participated in before—it was quite a contrast to the psalm-singing we did in our church. But it was Billy Sunday's preaching that kept Billy Frank sitting on the edge of his seat. Sunday waved, shouted, climbed on the pulpit and the piano, and looked and acted more like a baseball player than a preacher!

I suppose churchgoing after that seemed rather mild in comparison, but we were faithful in attending. It's true that Billy relieved the long hours in church with much heel-kicking and knuckle-cracking. He was quite a restless boy. And he did come to know the church building very well—every nook and cranny—with his after-church explorations while we visited with neighbors and friends.

The children never were made to go to church, they always went willingly. We attended Sunday school classes first, and we were never late, and I know that habit shows itself in Billy's life today. Billy can call me and say, "Mother, I'll be over at eleven o'clock to see you for a while," and I know that he'll be there exactly at that time, or in all probability fifteen minutes earlier. Billy has always been not only punctual, but early. As busy as he is, he is never late for anything. I suppose that habit was ingrained in him early in life. Because we were a farm family, there were always chores that had to be done very early in the morning.

We watched suburban Charlotte spread out. My husband's dream of having a milk route became reality. His business was growing. I was able to assist him with many of the countless details of record keeping and billing procedures—but the day for my husband, Billy and Melvin actually began as early as 2:30 each morning. At the peak of my husband's business they were milking as many as seventy-five cows. It was a hard life: getting up early, eating breakfast, and the boys would have to go off to school.

Children need to be taught early to work and accept responsibility. I knew if they couldn't accept responsibility as youngsters, they would have difficulty taking things on in later life. One of Billy Frank's first jobs was sweeping the big veranda which encircled our first home. Of course I was never quite certain what he would do with the broom, but he did have to be taught to share in the home responsibilities.

Catherine and Billy were real buddies. They liked nothing better than to ride their bicycles along dusty Park Road. I have often heard Billy in his sermons refer to the lessons he learned while learning to ride his two-wheeler. I can still see him getting on, starting out, falling off, getting back on and crashing into something. But he was determined. Today he says:

> I found there was one thing I had to do on that bike if I wanted to stay on it. I had to keep moving forward. If I stopped moving forward, I would fall off and hurt myself. A Christian must learn that. He must keep moving forward in his faith.

Melvin says one of his first recollections of Billy is seeing him riding down Park Road on his bicycle. Trailing along behind Billy were his small black goat, his large brown goat, and the pet collie.

Nothing pleased Billy more than to have a car happen along and everyone turn to look at him and laugh! I often stood at my living room window, watching the procession, and I had to laugh too. Billy Frank and Billy the goat were quite a team! Mr. Graham bought a beautiful little wagon and the prettiest little harness. Off the Billies would go. Billy had the goat trained to come to the back door, and he would stop until I'd throw out a piece of bread. Only then would he go on—he just wouldn't budge until he had the piece of bread! Sometimes Billy would have to call to me, "Hey, Mom, throw out the bread." When the goat got tired of the whole thing, in the manner of stubborn goats, he would just lie down and that was that! It was one problem Billy could never quite solve. But I cheerfully went along with the goat play and saved scraps of bread. I am thankful today for these happy memories.

CHAPTER THREE

The Bible Says ...

The fear of the Lord is the beginning of knowledge.
Proverbs 1:7, NIV

We moved into our new big red brick home in 1927, and in 1932 daughter Jean was born. When Jean was about six months old, I noticed she had a lump in the area of her throat. I told the doctor, but he said it was nothing to be alarmed about. When she was two and one-half years old she came down with a bad cold and in three days that little lump grew to be as large as a fist. It was purple and ugly looking and frightened me. It happened almost overnight. The doctor performed surgery and drained it and she recovered. The doctors didn't know what it was then, but it left a scar.

In the final months of the Hoover administration in early 1933, the country was in the throes of depression. The economic tailspin also hit us. My husband had always been a hard worker and very frugal. By careful management and real thrift he had savings in the bank. When Roosevelt became President, he declared a bank holiday. When the holiday was over, our bank failed to open its doors and our savings were wiped out.

Billy remembers it well. We'd experienced some financial disasters before—bad weather for the crops, hail, drought—but this was something else. It hit my husband hard and caused some discouragement.

It was about this time that my sister, Lil Barker, convinced me that I should take time out to attend a weekly Bible class. I have always been so grateful to my sister for urging me to do this. The result was revolutionary! Actually my sister and her husband had been praying for us for some time, although at the time we did not know this. When she suggested that I take time out to attend this Bible class, I thought, *Well, what is the need to go?* We went to Sunday school and church. Lil was honest with me and said, "Morrow, I sense that there is a need for you to get down deep into the Word and see what God really has to say to you." So I went.

I couldn't wait to get back the next week! The class had something I desperately wanted and needed more than anything else. I just couldn't wait. It made me really start delving into the Bible on my own, and I began to see things I'd never noticed before. I found myself staying up into the wee hours of the morning just reading the Bible.

Of course I was a busy mother and busy dairy farmer's wife, so there wasn't always time during the day to read and study, but I wouldn't have missed that Bible class for anything, once I started going. For six years I went every week, only missing two sessions. I was so eager to learn. Mrs. Whitted, a member of the First Presbyterian Church in Charlotte, taught that class. I attended that class faithfully for so many years. It was in the class that I came to understand that the Holy Spirit indwells a Christian's heart.

Ever since that realization, I have had a great yearning to help others believe in the working of the Holy Spirit. For so long I did not know that the Holy Spirit is really here to do work in *my life*; not the other person's life, but in *my life*. It comes down to the individual, and it was the most wonderful realization of my life to see how the Lord was working things out in our lives as a family.

It was about this time that I convinced Mr. Graham that we should both attend a Brethren Bible Class at night. I suspect that meant more to the two of us spiritually than almost anything that came into our lives.

Between the two of us we devoured our Scofield Bibles and I started ordering Christian books from a New York mail-order house. I became an avid reader, and then I made it a practice to see to it that there were always good books lying around the house for the children to read.

During those early years I read something from the Proverbs every day and always read the Psalms. Then I learned to love the older prophets, and the New Testament, of course.

In between all of this I went through the usual ordeals of a mother with her growing family. Billy always had so much energy. One day, in desperation, I hustled him off to the family doctor. I remember sighing wearily and saying, "He's got too much energy. He never wears down."

The doctor examined Billy Frank carefully and said, "He's perfectly normal, Mrs. Graham, it's just the way he's built." It was a prophetic statement, as the years since have shown.

People have asked me on more than one occasion if the children ever fought. Catherine recalls plenty of scraps. I came home one day to find out that they had waged war over so simple a thing as a can of beans! It didn't seem to matter to Billy at the time that Catherine was younger than he and a girl besides. He actually pushed her through two sets of swinging doors. Melvin would tell you that there were plenty of times he regarded Billy Frank as more of an adversary than a big brother hero!

Billy was always full of pranks; sometimes he carried things a bit too far, and off came his father's belt. Mr. Graham never punished in anger or desperation, but when he did see the necessity for correction, I winced. At such times I had to remind myself of another Proverb: "*Do not withhold discipline from a child; if you punish him with the rod, he will not die*" (Proverbs 23:13, NIV). More than once I wiped tears from my eyes and turned my head so the children wouldn't see, but I always stood behind my husband when he administered discipline. I knew he was doing what was biblically correct. And the children didn't die!

We were both reassured by Proverbs 13:24: "*He who spares the rod hates his son, but he who loves him is careful to discipline him,*" (NIV). In later years it was an encouragement for us as parents to hear Billy say on many occasions that the Book of Proverbs is one of his favorite Bible sections.

Billy has preached some fine messages on the influence of a godly home through the years. Understandably my husband's heart and my own were deeply moved as we heard him say the things that we tried to put into practice in our home.

My husband and I established a family altar the day we were married and we carried that through. In the breakfast room I always kept a Scripture calendar with a verse and the comment for the day. Each morning we read that, too, and prayed to the Lord. As we gathered at the breakfast table, everyone would bow his head and fold his hands as my husband asked the blessing.

Billy has often said in his preaching:

Take God into your partnership. There ought to be a family altar in your home. God holds the man responsible for the spiritual life in the home. You are the preacher in your home. You are to set the example. If there is no altar, if there are no prayers, and if no grace is said at the table, it is the man's fault.

Mr. Graham set a good example in our home. Often, as I packed the children's school lunches, I could hear my husband talking to the children. He helped them memorize literally hundreds of Bible verses. Every week they were expected to learn Scripture verses.

I looked forward to our evenings together as a family. Everyone gathered in the family room. We did this right after dinner dishes were put away. It was the most important thing in our life, this time of Bible reading and prayer. I know that today Billy recalls those instructional periods as among the most important in his life, helping him to become saturated with the Bible. In preaching, he quotes from passages and verses he learned when we gathered together as a family at the family altar.

Each of our children, in one way or another, has thanked us many times over for our times of family devotions. They have said that these times together taught them what they wouldn't have learned on their own.

There are numerous passages in the Bible that speak to us of the importance of leading our children into a knowledge of the Word of God. Mr. Graham and I wanted the children to grow up to know and honor the Word of God. We recognized that if this was to happen, they would need to hear the Word of the Lord spoken and discussed within our home. It was a burning desire in my life and in my heart, that our children would know the Lord. When we turn children loose from the home, sometimes they find the Lord, but often times they don't. I did not want to run that risk with our children. The home is the place to receive training from the Word of God.

As I view the situation in the world—crime, immorality, rebellious youth, a weakening family life, and the prevailing conditions throughout the land—I feel very strongly that if Deuteronomy 6:4–7 were practiced by parents, we would see far less unrest and problems in the world. This entire sixth chapter speaks to me of God-given home life and was most important in the bringing up of our children.

> *... The Lord our God, the Lord is one. Love the Lord your God with all your heart and with all your soul and with all your strength. These commandments that I give you today are to be upon your hearts. Impress them on your children. Talk about*

them when you sit at home and when you walk along the road, when you lie down and when you get up, (NIV).

My burden for the women of the world is the same that Billy proclaims wherever he goes: that they will come to know Christ as their Savior, then get into Bible study and carry out the teachings of the Word of God in the daily experiences of their lives.

I certainly never thought that one of our children would become a Christian leader, recognized worldwide, when we as a family knelt to pray and when we gathered together every evening to read the Bible. The Lord has done so much for Billy. We recognize that, but God wants to do the same for each of us. God is no respecter of persons.

Through the years, as I have seen and heard Billy preach, I have watched as he holds up the Bible and says, "The Bible says … " That is an expression he uses often. I am thankful Billy Frank heard it repeated in our home.

The Bible says, "*A wise son heeds his father's instruction*" (Proverbs 13:1, NIV).

In our family we were accustomed to getting down on our knees together to pray, and we expected the Lord to answer our prayers. Our faith in those days was really strong. When the children were little they prayed for their dogs, cats, everything—but they were learning to pray and we had so many answers to prayer. My faith was always greatly strengthened by these big answers and little answers.

But, have you ever tried to pray and the words would not come? Have you known times when your heart was so heavy and the anxiety so great that it was all you could do to cry out to the Father? I have also had those times. I knew that David the psalmist had those moments also. This was comforting to me. I also had the reassurance that God understood.

My favorite devotional book through the years has been Amy Carmichael's book, *Edges of His Ways*. In one of her daily devotionals I was pointed to Psalm 38:9. *"Lord, all my desire is before You; and my sighing is not hidden from You."* Amy Carmichael wrote that as she read those words of David it was as if God, who is never far away, said, *What does it matter about words, when all thy desire is before Me?*

None of us will ever forget the time when we knelt to pray without my husband there beside us. Mr. Graham was struck in the face by a piece of wood flying from a saw. It was very, very serious. He hovered between life and death for two days. The doctors were certain he would die. Surgeons were called in and had to perform a very dangerous operation on his face. He was in bad shape.

My Bible class friends joined in prayer. Our daughter, Jean, was only three months old. I remember going up to our bedroom and just laying hold of the Lord. I know I groaned as I pleaded with God to restore my husband to us, once again in perfect health. We needed him so!

By the third morning his eyes looked clearer and he seemed more normal. I got down on my knees beside his bed and thanked the Lord for answered prayer. I knew Frank was going to get well, for the Lord gave me perfect assurance about it. In Psalm 138:3 I read: "*In the day when I cried out, You answered me, And made me bold with strength in my soul.*"

Mr. Graham did get well. It was a remarkable answer to prayer that the children, my husband and I never forgot. The Lord was doing a work in Mr. Graham's and my life through all of this. I wouldn't take anything today for all those experiences.

Twelve years later, we found ourselves again as a family on our knees in prayer, pleading for the Lord to spare our daughter Jean's life. She came down with polio of the throat when an epidemic of bulbar-type polio swept through the city of Charlotte. She was placed in isolation and quarantined for three weeks. The first forty-eight hours were the most critical. We were told she probably wouldn't live. There were two other patients with the same bulbar paralysis Jean had. They both died the third day. That frightened us, but I kept telling my husband, "Frank, we have the Lord." And again, the Lord answered prayer in a marvelous way.

Since the children have married and gone their separate ways, and since my husband's death, I have found myself with more time to devote to prayer. I pray without ceasing for Billy and the tremendous responsibility that God has given to him; but also for my other children, my thirteen grandchildren, fourteen great-grandchildren (at the time of this writing), and for worldwide needs.

I often wonder if we, as mothers, recognize how much our prayers have influenced our children's choices through life. It is something we should contemplate seriously. As I look at my own life, I know better than anyone how much weakness and failure there has been. Yet, we try—as mothers we must try and keep on trying. Then we must seek God's face and His mercy as we trust Him to forgive those times when we have failed Him and our children, and ask Him to bring good out of evil.

There are some things I would do differently if I had the years to live over, but as I recall the long hours and the hard work, the thing that stands out is the fact that we surely did read the Bible and pray. As busy as we were, and as tired as we often were, still we were diligent in this. I believe that did make a difference. We have a great God, One who lavishes blessings unto His children's children. He is a God who keeps His Word.

The Bible says: "*The wise woman builds her house ...* " (Proverbs 14:1, NIV), and "*The house of the wicked will be overthrown: but the tent of the upright will flourish*" (Proverbs 14:11).

Today we find in many homes that children are given first place. That may seem right in some respects, but it isn't God's way; that is, not according to Scripture. When we get away from what the Bible says, we are in trouble. "*The righteous man walks in his integrity; his children are blessed after him*" (Proverbs 20:7).

Proverbs also tells us that "*There is a generation that curses its father, and does not bless its mother*" (Proverbs 30:11). Mr. Graham and I did not want that to happen in our family.

We expected the children to be clean and moral, and never doubted that they would be. They knew this, and Billy has been quoted as saying, "Our parents trusted us and we wanted to live up to their confidence in us."

We knew there was only one right way to live, and it was all laid out for us in the Bible. It's how we tried to live, and how we wanted them to learn to live.

Every word of God is pure; He is a shield to those that put their trust in him.

Proverbs 30:5

CHAPTER FOUR

Mother, I Am a Changed Boy!

Trust in the Lord with all your heart; and lean not on your own understanding. In all your ways acknowledge Him, and He shall direct your paths.

Proverbs 3:5–6

The year 1934 stands out significantly for our family. It was to prove to be particularly meaningful for Billy Frank.

Mr. Graham and a number of other Christian laymen met one day in our pasture. Spiritual apathy had moved upon the Charlotte citizenry during Depression days. It was of more than a little concern to some of the local Christian businessmen. The complacent churchgoers of Charlotte needed a fire kindled in their hearts. Who better could do this than the well-known, fiery Southern evangelist Mordecai Ham? And so these men, including my husband, met together in one of our pastures to look the scene over and to pray.

But the men weren't the only ones concerned; so were we women. While the men met, I had an all-day prayer meeting and Bible study in our home. In spite of local clerical opposition on the part of some, and a guarded neutrality on the part of other ministers, the invitation went out to the evangelist. Before long these same businessmen were erecting a large tabernacle of raw pine. For eleven weeks, beginning in September 1934, the meetings were to go on with Mordecai Ham holding the audiences spellbound. Included in that audience one memorable night was our son Billy.

Billy was now sixteen and just beginning his senior year in high school. Two of the first verses I ever had Billy commit to memory were Proverbs 3:5, 6. Now those verses were to become meaningful to his young heart.

Vernon Patterson, one of the men who led the meeting in our pasture when they discussed getting Mordecai Ham to hold the revival meetings, had prayed very pointedly that "out of Charlotte the Lord would raise up someone to preach the Gospel to the ends of the earth." I still find it an awesome thing to realize that God answered that prayer and chose to do so by putting Billy under conviction and sending him forward to walk that sawdust aisle and trust in the Lord with all his heart.

Billy actually went to the meeting upon the urging of the McMakin boys, and also, I'm sure, out of some curiosity. But God was working out His plan for Billy Frank's life and I was just so thankful that he was going. Yes, I saw him go forward, and my mother-heart was beating very fast. I was just rejoicing. I felt it was a wonderful thing to do, but my emotional experience was yet to come.

When we arrived home that night from the meeting, Billy was already home in the breakfast room, pretending to make a sandwich. When I came in he threw his arms around me and said, "Mother, I'm a changed boy!"

I wept tears of joy into my pillow that night. Both Mr. Graham and I knew that this was what Billy himself in later years was to call his hour of decision. In the days that turned into weeks and then months, Billy's words were to prove true. One of the verses that Billy had learned was John 3:16: "*For God so loved the world, that He gave His only begotten Son, that whoever believes in Him should not perish but have everlasting life.*" Whether or not Billy as a sixteen-year-old fully understood *all* the implications of that, I do not know, but I do know that he was, as he so graphically described it, "a changed boy."

My son Melvin has often recalled those days following Billy's new-birth experience. Melvin in particular had opportunity, day by day, to see the change this wrought in his brother. The two of them worked together in the fields and with the dairy. Melvin, however, was always more interested in the dairy than Billy was. Billy would milk, and he would always help, but Melvin put a lot more vim and energy into it right from the start, even though he was six years younger than Billy.

I can look back now and see how the Lord was preparing Billy for what he is doing today; and he was preparing Melvin too. In those days we used mules to plow our fields. Melvin remembers the day they were out in the field plowing and they saw a little plane skywriting. It was advertising something, and the initials were GPG. Billy said immediately, "Melvin, that means 'Go preach the Gospel.'" Melvin says he turned to Billy and answered, "No, that means 'Go plow the ground!'"

Change was evident in more ways than one, and noticed by many individuals. Grady Wilson, a friend who followed Billy up the sawdust trail that memorable night, remembers their early efforts at witnessing through their school Bible Club. For the most part, those who recall those first attempts considered Billy shy and very nervous, but he was anxious to share. He wasn't considered a sanctimonious saint by his teachers and school contemporaries (although there were some schoolmates who, in the way of unthinking youth, jeered at him from time to time), but he was noticeably more thoughtful, kinder, and quieter. Even in little things it was very evident that something tremendous had happened inside him—he had indeed changed!

CHAPTER FIVE

A Testing Time

Cast all your anxiety on him because he cares for you.
1 Peter 5:7, NIV

The month of March before Billy's high school graduation, Billy's homeroom teacher stopped at the house one day and said, "Mrs. Graham, I'm so sorry to have to tell you this, but Billy is not going to make the grade."

I remember just staring at the teacher. I was so stunned. Then I said, "Oh, no, that can't be."

The teacher looked back at me so kindly and said, "Yes, it is true. He's losing his strength and his grades are very poor. Mrs. Graham, I think the boy is working too hard and trying to study, and he just can't do it. Every morning at eleven o'clock he just falls asleep in class."

When she went out the door, I felt like I had just been chopped through the heart. I turned back into the living room and prayed, "Oh, Lord, that can't be true. You'll just have to do something." At Christmastime, Billy had read ten or eleven historical books from the library. I remember finishing that prayer by saying, "Lord, You are preparing him and You are educating him for something. I don't know what it is, but it's up to You, and it's Your problem."

This was a great test of my faith; but God saw Billy Frank through! I left that problem with the Lord, and by the end of the school year, when he was seventeen, he made his grades and graduated with his class.

Melvin and Jean were *A* students. Billy and Catherine were the ones reading all the time—and not always their studies— but they were just average students.

I sensed in that strange way known to mothers that the days ahead for Billy Frank would be of tremendous importance. How was I to pray for this son of mine?

Billy's favorite spot for reading was right in the middle of the living room floor. He'd lie on his back, put his feet up, and read. Sometimes when he comes home now, he takes off his coat, gets down on the floor the same way and reads. Billy hasn't changed a whole lot. I remember a few years ago he did that, and as I stepped around him I recall looking back and down at him, saying, "Billy Frank, you haven't changed at all since you were twelve years old!"

The change in Billy had been so dramatic that it strongly influenced his decision to go to a Bible school following graduation. All those years I had been praying—perhaps as a somewhat selfish mother—that the Lord would lead Billy either to Wheaton College or to Moody Bible Institute. Now I found myself praying with even more urgency; I couldn't bear the thought of him going anywhere else, and I actually didn't want to hear anyplace else.

Evangelist Jimmie Johnson had come to Charlotte for some meetings. He influenced the thinking of Grady and T. W. Wilson, Billy's friends, so they decided to attend Bob Jones College. I still clung to my hopes that Billy could go to Wheaton, but it was so far away and much more expensive. When it finally came time for the decision to be made, I agreed that he should go to Cleveland, Tennessee, with the Wilson brothers.

Once again, I found much comfort and help in the Bible as Amy Carmichael nudged my thinking.

Even so, Father: for so it seemed good in Your sight.

Matthew 11:26

"Even so, Father" in Aramaic is, "O yes, my Father, for such is Your will"—the "Yes" of complete content, the welcoming "Yes" of acceptance. He asks us: *Are you pleased with my will?*—

not, Are you going to bear up under it and not show your real feelings?

We all know what it is to plan a pleasure for a child and then watch to see its pleasure. Some of us know what it is to plan the best our love can think of, which yet may be, naturally speaking, a disappointment to the child; and we know how we watch for its response. Love is planning for us. Love has planned the best that Love could plan. Perhaps we cannot help one another more than by praying that we may never disappoint our Father's faith in us, but always follow our blessed Lord in this as in everything, and answer His trust with the words, "O yes, Father." "*Are you pleased with My will, My child?*" "O yes, my Father."

My husband packed Billy Frank and Grady and T.W., with all their luggage, into our Plymouth and headed toward the Appalachians, a day's drive west. When my husband returned, I said to him, "Frank, honey, Billy has left the home fires. He has been accustomed to opening the Word of God every day and praying; I believe that he will continue to do so. Even if he continues to read only a verse a day, I believe that God is going to use him. Let's have the faith to believe and ask God to continue to work in Billy's heart."

God gave me tremendous faith then and I was persistent in

my praying. Every day when Mr. Graham was not pressed on the farm, he joined me, and we would go up to our bedroom after lunch and get down on our knees and pray for Billy. We felt it was necessary. We claimed that verse, *"Be diligent to present yourself approved unto God, a worker who does not need to be ashamed, rightly dividing the word of truth"* (2 Timothy 2:15). We prayed that prayer for Billy for seven years.

Billy hadn't made his mind up to be an evangelist when he went away to school, but he had only been away about six weeks when he wrote home saying, "Mother, I think the Lord is calling me to the ministry, and if He does, it will be in the field of evangelism. That's the thing I'm the most interested in."

A few weeks after that he wrote home for a particular set of books. I praised the Lord for that! I said to Mr. Graham, "We'll live on bread and water to send him those books." I knew then that Billy was really thinking along deep spiritual lines, and I started praising the Lord for what he was going to do. I knew there was something special or he wouldn't have wanted those books. They were the C. H. Mackintosh books from England, which Billy had been seeing me read for years. I never took a book and said, "Here, you read this," and forced anything like that on the children. That would only have led to rebellion; but God marvelously opened the way and He led.

At Christmastime Billy came home. He had really exhausted his strength during those few months and fought a running battle with the flu. The studies and strenuous schedule from early morning until late at night combined with other factors, not the least of which was Billy's respiratory troubles, indicated to us that after the first semester Billy should go to a Bible school in Florida. Billy needed the sunshine and warmer climate, and the Florida Bible Institute at Temple Terrace, near Tampa, was highly recommended.

CHAPTER SIX

Answered Prayer

Now this is the confidence that we have in Him, that if we ask anything according to His will, He hears us. And if we know that He hears us, whatever we ask, we know that we have the petitions that we have asked of Him.

1 John 5:14, 15

It was at Florida that Billy Frank really found his gift. We drove him to the Florida Bible Institute with high anticipation, and we were not disappointed when we got there. I thought it was the prettiest place I had ever seen, with the most magnificent buildings. It had at one time been a millionaire's resort estate. The grounds were gorgeous. I thought we couldn't leave Billy in a more beautiful spot, and you could feel the wonderful Christian influence there.

Billy's letters started arriving. They were so refreshing! He always wrote once or twice every week. Billy appreciated my letters too, and I wrote him often. I kept the home fires burning for him and he sensed it.

When he first went away to school I prayed, "Lord, don't

allow me to write any letters to Billy that won't be an encouragement to him. Let everything I write really be a help to him in the things that pertain to Yourself." I believe the Lord was faithful in answering that prayer request.

One of the first letters from Florida said, "I especially appreciate the sweet, cheerful letters you write me."

Another letter said, "Mother, words can't express Florida Bible Institute. ... I've never felt so close to God in my life. This is the first time I have really enjoyed studying the Word of God. ... I love it here."

At the Institute his friendship with the dean, John Minder, deepened. Opportunities for preaching arose, and Billy began practicing his sermons on squirrels and rabbits out on the golf course. Every little circumstance seemed to draw him closer to the Lord, and his letters were precious to me as he recounted how the Lord was working in his life. You didn't make long-distance telephone calls in those days—at least country people like us didn't—and so Billy's letters, so full of affection, were treasured by me and my heart was filled to overflowing. Surely God was answering our prayers in wonderful ways.

Billy was not only busy studying, but he also took on jobs to help with expenses. He helped with mowing lawns on campus; he even did some shining of shoes, and carrying bags for visiting conference speakers such as Gipsy Smith, Homer

Rodeheaver, W. B. Riley, William Evans and other well-known evangelicals. One letter he wrote to me mentioned that he was shining the shoes of one of these great men. He looked up into the man's face and thought, *Oh, if some day I could just be a great preacher like him!*

The subject of Billy's thinking in every letter was the Lord. Another letter, which touched Mr. Graham and me very much, revealed a deepening relationship with the Lord and a new maturity, a fuller growing-up process.

First I want to say I rededicated my life to the Lord Jesus Christ last night under the stars. Mother, I've been in tears for weeks under conviction for my past indifference. I want to ask you and Daddy's forgiveness because God has already forgiven. But every time I go to these great meetings I think of Daddy because he loves that kind of meeting so much.

All the big men come here from the north. Dr. Herbert Lockyer was here recently. Another special conference meeting begins tomorrow. It will be that way all the time. ...

I am working a little everyday so as to help on my expenses. ... I'm much stronger and feel good. ... I need a little more money to finish out the month. ...

As I think about it now, it seems incredible, but we sent Billy only six dollars a month for spending money and expenses. That's unbelievable, isn't it? There were times when I could have slipped him money in my letters, but I knew Mr. Graham didn't want me to do it. Billy had to learn the value of money, and he surely did. I remember one time he went over to see my older sister who was living in nearby Orlando. He borrowed a dollar and a half from her over the weekend. He just had to have some clean shirts and didn't have a cent. I think a lot of times Billy Frank didn't have a cent.

In January of 1938 Billy wrote a letter which revealed that his girl friend was having second thoughts about him.

> ... but it's all in the hands of the Lord and I don't worry about it. God is directing my life and He will do the very best for those who leave the choice to Him. ... I am not going to think of getting married for a long time to come—I have four years of schooling at least ahead of me. I know the Lord led me to enter school here, and I can say with great certainty that I am His servant. There is nothing between the Lord and me.

He was also concerned now about his grades and we knew he was striving to make good ones. "My grades are not out yet, but they will be sent to you as soon as possible. ... "

On Sundays he held street-corner services when he wasn't preaching in some church. At first he had to create opportunities for preaching, but soon he began to become known as Young Graham, who "does not mince words when he tells church members they are headed for the same hell as the bootlegger and racketeer unless they get right and live right for God."

He was made a chaplain to the trailer parks. He visited prisoners and had discussion groups with them. His letters again revealed his busyness and the great satisfaction and blessing he was experiencing.

It seems I enjoy letters from home more than ever before.

I preached Saturday night to a larger crowd than usual. Sunday it seemed that heaven opened and fell on the meeting. Never have I preached with such freedom. Sunday morning five rededicated their lives to the Lord, and Sunday afternoon five grown men made a profession of faith in our blessed Savior. Sunday night two grown young people found Christ. Several said it was one of the best days the Tabernacle had seen in a long time.

At that time Billy was assistant pastor of a Christian Missionary Alliance Church. His letter continued:

God forbid that I should boast only in Him. I can certainly feel the prayers of my loved ones at home. And how I long to see you all again, but I'm in His service now and I must stay until the last of the summer. ...

When the break between him and his girl friend came, Billy reacted in a way that I knew God would bless. He sought counsel from his good friend Dr. John Minder. To us he wrote: "How wonderful it is to have that peace that passes understanding, and how I love the Lord for what he has done for me."

This was one of Billy's first "furnace" experiences. His character was being forged; it was a necessary part of his learning about life and the heartaches and disillusionment that comes to all of us at one time or another and in different ways. Isaiah 43 became meaningful to him:

> *... Fear not, for I have redeemed you, I have summoned you by name; you are mine. When you pass through the waters, I will be with you; and when you pass through the rivers, they will not sweep over you. When you walk through the fire, you will not be burned; the flames will not set you ablaze. For I am the Lord, your God. ...*

Isaiah 43:1–3, NIV

Billy realized now more than ever that he had a purpose, an objective, a call. His letters, which had always been serious, now began to show even more clearly that he had but one passion: He had to proclaim the Gospel. He himself has said, "I had but one passion, and that was to win souls. I didn't have a passion to be a great preacher; I had a passion to win souls. I'd never been trained to be a public speaker. I had to learn in the best way I knew."

Billy's destiny was decided.

My long-awaited answer to prayer came when Billy entered Wheaton in the fall of 1940. He had graduated in May from the Florida Bible Institute, and he arrived at Wheaton an ordained Baptist minister. Billy had matured during those four years away from home. Now he was twenty-one. He now had the grounding in the Bible that we so earnestly prayed he would receive. He himself said of those years that it was there he:

> ... learned the importance of the Bible and came to believe with all my heart in its full inspiration. It became a rapier and a sword in my hand that I have used as a hammer as well as a sword to break open the hearts of men and to direct them to the Lord Jesus Christ.

That summer he and a friend had rattled their way to York, Pennsylvania, to conduct evangelistic meetings. The pastor there had publicized Billy and his friend as "Youth Aflame for God."

No one could have been happier than I, however, when the fall term opened. Up until this time Billy had always corresponded with regularity, but that was to change while at Wheaton. While we missed those letters, we knew that he was so busy studying and preaching that he really didn't have time to write as often. We had observed that every little circumstance seemed to draw Billy closer to the Lord; he used these experiences to deepen his relationship with Christ.

One letter he did write was tremendously important, and I will never forget what he said. The letter told about meeting Ruth Bell, whom he later married, and he said, "Mother, the reason I like Ruth so much is that she looks and reminds me of you." I thought that was such a compliment; then, when I finally did get to meet Ruth, I was really touched—Ruth is far above me!

Ruth spent many of her growing-up years in the Orient where her Father, Dr. Nelson Bell, was a surgeon in a Presbyterian missionary hospital. Ruth had many admirers; she was not only beautiful to look at, but the beauty of her Christian character was exactly what every mother wishes for her son. When Billy brought her home the first summer after Wheaton to meet us, we loved her immediately. Then on August 13, 1943, when she became Billy's bride, I couldn't thank the Lord enough for giving Billy Frank someone who was so right for him.

We followed Ruth and Billy's marriage with concern and interest. Concern because Billy's dedication was of such intensity that I, as his mother, wondered if he could maintain the pace he was carrying. By this time he was pastor of the Village Church in Western Springs, twenty miles southwest of Chicago, and he became the speaker on the radio program "Songs in the Night." This was a forty-five minute program of preaching and singing on one of Chicago's powerful stations at 10:15 on Sunday nights. We couldn't get the program on our house radio, so Mr. Graham and I sat in the car and tuned the radio dial until the station came in loud and clear. Then we sat back marveling and we'd say to each other, "Imagine, that's our Billy Frank!"

CHAPTER SEVEN

Revival Fire

Commit your way to the Lord; trust also in Him;
and He shall bring it to pass.

Psalm 37:5

A mother shares in a peculiar way in the crises times that come into the lives of her sons and daughters. She need not even be near that child to sense when that son or daughter is going through a time of soul-searching. Such is the motherly instinct, God-given, which resides in the hearts of us as mothers.

Billy tells of being in Southern California the last of August 1949, and of his first encounter with Dr. Henrietta Mears (who has since gone to be with the Lord). He met her at Forest Home, the well-known Christian conference center founded by Miss Mears. Miss Mears, known around the world as one of the greatest Christian educators, was lovingly called Teacher by all who knew her. Billy confided in this remarkable woman and shared some of his fears with her. His first Los Angeles campaign lay just ahead of him—the campaign that was to go down in history as the event that actually launched Billy into his worldwide ministry.

God used Miss Mears to listen to Billy pour out his troubled thoughts, and years later Billy was to say of her:

> She has had a remarkable influence, both directly and indirectly, on my life. In fact, I doubt if any other woman outside of my wife and mother has had such a marked influence. Her gracious spirit, her devotional life, her steadfastness for the simple Gospel, and her knowledge of the Bible have been a continual inspiration and amazement to me. She is certainly one of the greatest Christians I have ever known.

In the fall of 1957 it was my special joy to meet Dr. Mears, whose path so providentially crossed Billy's at the time he faced that crisis in his soul. Billy was being featured on the "This Is Your Life" television program and we flew to the West Coast. Miss Mears hosted a party for Billy and Ruth; there were 250 invited guests, Christians from all over the United States. I had the opportunity to thank her personally for what she had done for Billy and what she meant to him. There are times, indeed, when we can only share from a distance what goes on in our children's lives, but isn't it wonderful that God, in His mercy and goodness, has others who can minister with love and understanding? Such a person was Dr. Henrietta Mears.

There have been others—many, many others—whose lives have greatly influenced Billy's and Billy has always been quick to acknowledge such influences. Mr. Graham and I had the privilege, therefore, from time to time to meet some of these marvelous men and women of God. Billy has always possessed a sweetness and genuine humility; he is no respecter of persons. He is as much at ease and at home with royalty and presidents and their wives, as he is with members of his own family. Billy, as a youngster and later as a teenager, was actually quite shy. He has admitted to this publicly and in his writings. So God has done a wonderful thing in his life in this regard.

Billy has always taken very seriously the position that has been thrust upon him of ministering and counseling to those whom the world considers great. God has dealt very graciously through Billy when he has been called upon and invited to the White House, when he has conducted private church services for the queen of England, and when he has met with the Pope, cardinals, bishops, emperors, business executives, Hollywood stars, television celebrities, and others in positions of world leadership and prominence.

I entertained Mr. and Mrs. Richard Nixon at tea. Billy had visited Mr. Nixon's mother during her illness and so Billy said to Mr. Nixon that it was only fair that Mr. Nixon visit me. Mr. Nixon wanted to see what our dairy farm was like, and they wanted to come. The Nixons were so cordial. She was so lovely. Mr. Nixon said to me, "I'm visiting you in your red brick house and you must come visit me in my White House," and we laughed about it because at the time he wasn't president yet. When he was elected about a year later, we were invited to a Sunday service at the White House. Billy preached that Sunday and afterwards we were guests in the second floor living quarters.

You must understand that this was a thrill for this "country woman" from North Carolina. Mrs. Nixon was such a gracious hostess and the reception was just beautiful. While we were admiring the rooms, she did such a homey thing. She went over to the sofa in front of one of the windows, picked up the drapery and said, "I tell you, we need draperies so badly. ..." The lower part of the drape, hidden by the sofa, was in threads. "I keep the sofa there to hide it," she added. We thought it a warm, natural thing for her to do. The White House was indescribable. It was one of the highlights in all my experiences.

All that has happened to the Nixons in more recent years has been hurtful to us, just as it's been hurtful to almost everybody else. You would have to be very insensitive not to have feelings about those events.

I also met Lady Bird Johnson when she was in Charlotte. My daughters and I were very impressed with her graciousness. When the Johnsons were in the White House, Billy and Ruth spent time with them also. Actually Billy has been a frequent visitor in Washington; he prays with those who request prayer, and counsels with those who seek direction from the Bible. Billy's friendship with presidents and politicians is not because of politics. The Bible says very plainly that prayers, intercessions, and giving of thanks, is to be made for all men.

The story of the "Christ for Greater Los Angeles" campaign and Billy's preaching there is so well known that it doesn't need repeating. Dr. Charles E. Fuller of the "Old Fashioned Revival Hour" broadcast at that time made a prophetic statement. He said, "Truly the hand of God is upon our brother Graham."

Billy phoned us from Los Angeles three times, begging Daddy and me to come. "If you knew how the Holy Spirit was working out here, you would just get on the first plane," he pleaded. But Mr. Graham never enjoyed trips—he just didn't like to travel—and I wouldn't go without him.

I was so thankful that Billy had always been eager and able to learn from others, for now he would need the competent help and able advice of those who knew far more than he about all the mechanics involved in conducting citywide crusades. Willis Haymaker became Billy's first crusade director, setting up and supervising crusades across the country and around the world in subsequent years. Willis and his wife endeared themselves to me; he became known as the elder statesman of the Team.

It had been a long time since a religious revival made the news bulletins; it was, therefore, nothing short of a very humbling experience for us in Charlotte to realize that this was Billy Frank they were talking about. When Billy first went into Youth for Christ work and I observed his busy schedule, the throngs of people at the meetings, and the stresses to which he was subject, I claimed Jeremiah 23:23 for Billy. God told the ancient prophet: '*Am I only a God nearby ... and not a God far away?*' (NIV). I knew God had a long arm; He was wholly trustworthy. I have always had great confidence in the Lord's watch-care over Billy, and I have not feared, therefore, for his life.

At that time Billy said to the press, and wrote the same thing to us: "I feel so undeserving of all the Spirit has done, because the work has been God's and not man's. I want no credit or glory. I want the Lord Jesus to have it all." I may sound like a very prejudiced mother who can see no fault in her child, but I believe God has honored Billy all these years because he has consistently maintained that kind of an attitude and right spirit.

Billy and the Team—which by then included Tedd Smith, Grady Wilson, George Wilson, George Beverly Shea and Cliff Barrows—were constantly on the move. It's a good thing the Lord gave each of these men such understanding wives, for they would need to recognize their husband's place (and their own) in God's great plan. The wives did join their husbands from time to time at the various crusades, but these were young men with growing families. I was so very proud of Billy's wife, Ruth, who voiced the feelings of the others when she said:

> A mother, like the Lord, needs to be a very present help in times of trouble. A mother has to be with the children. Personally I love it. There are times when I wish we could be a more normal family; but God never asks us to give up one thing without giving so much in return that you wind up almost ashamed for yourself (for feeling that way).

The team could not have functioned as they did (and as they do) were it not for the sacrifice and understanding of these wives and children.

As I sat in the audience at the London Crusade, I could not help but shake my head in amazement. I'd been in some of Billy's other crusades, but this was quite special for me because we were in England. It would never cease to amaze me, however, regardless where a crusade was being held, that such immense crowds should come to hear Billy Frank. Billy himself has often said the explanation lies in the fact that people everywhere are desperately searching for personal peace and happiness and some understanding of the future.

As I sat there in London, I thought back and realized that an ocean and two decades separated Billy and me from the first sermon I'd ever heard him preach. But I discovered, with something of a surprise, that the effects were actually quite similar!

That first time, Mr. Graham and I had driven Billy to a little Baptist church about forty miles from Charlotte. It was Christmastime, and Billy was home from college. I knew that I was considerably more nervous than Billy, for I was just wet with cold perspiration. He was only in his late teens! To this day I don't remember one word he spoke. I do recall that we all commented about how good he was, but we all thought he was awfully loud!

Billy's sisters, Catherine and Jean, and his brother Melvin, remember that occasion as well. We all squirmed a bit uncomfortably, and afterwards we questioned one another about whether or not Billy talked too loud and fast! Catherine teased Billy a bit and told him, "Billy, you came out like you were preaching to a thousand people. My, you were loud!"

Jean reminded Billy that he wasn't preaching at Diamond Park (that was the trailer park in Florida near the Bible Institute) and that he wasn't talking to the animals out on the golf course! Billy took that so good-naturedly.

Every member of the family was already proud of Billy, if not somewhat overawed by his forcefulness and the way people—even in that little Baptist church that day—responded to his message. He was loud, I had to agree, and I told him so. I also told him, "Billy, you are convincing!" Billy's fervor has always been of such intensity that he could not restrain himself.

Once again thankfulness flooded over my entire being as I read the newspaper accounts:

> Billy takes the Bible and preaches it in simplicity, with clarity and urgency. He has no magic, no magnetism, he makes no appeal to the emotions. His power—and power he has—is in his indivisible conviction that he knows the right way of life, in his unassailable belief that the "Spirit of Christ" must drive away all unhappiness from the heart of the individual and break down the evil

that seeks to destroy the world. ... He punches out the facts—the facts that he reads out from the open Bible in his hand, and which he asks his audience to read again and again in their Bibles.

In more recent years, I have watched the crusades on television. People often ask, "How do you feel when you sit in an audience, or when you see Billy on TV?" My answer is always the same: I feel wonderful, and I sit in awe when I think of the great things the Lord has done.

People also want to know how I feel when Billy is misquoted or criticized. It doesn't bother me, and it doesn't bother him, either. You see, Mr. Graham and I always told the children the important thing is to be right in the eyes of God. God sees into our hearts. He reads motives. We know Billy commits everything unto the Lord. The Bible says, "*Trust in the Lord, and do good. ... Delight yourself also in the Lord, and He shall give you the desires of your heart*" (Psalm 37:3–4).

In the closing days of that London Crusade, Billy said:

All of you who have been here have become aware, I'm sure, that the atmosphere has been charged with the power of the Holy Spirit. ... I have felt like a spectator standing on the side watching God at work, and I wanted to get out of it as much as I could and just let Him take over ...

That is the way I have seen God at work in these crusades around the world. It is by His Holy Spirit; Billy is just a channel. Whether he is crusading in London, Africa, the Orient, the Far East, South America or North America, Billy and the message remain the same, true to the Word of God. It is always as one might say, "fit for a queen," and we are all royalty when we are in God's family.

CHAPTER EIGHT

The Life That Can Pray

The prayer of a righteous man is
powerful and effective.
James 5:16, NIV

Mr. Graham was with the Lord. In August of 1962 my husband of forty-six years passed away. He had high blood pressure, and for eighteen months preceding his death had had several strokes. I was so thankful that at the time of his death Billy was in the country.

Once again God proved Himself to be all that we needed as a family as we faced the death of our loved one together. In Billy's book *Peace with God* he reminds the reader that Jesus said He would never leave us, or forsake us.

Remember Jesus promised us that after he left the earth He would send Another—the Third Person of the Trinity—the Holy Spirit, who is called a Comforter (which actually means "one that helps alongside") that He may abide with us forever (see John 14:16).

My beloved Frank was gone; but the Holy Spirit—the Comforter—was there.

I remembered other words Billy had spoken:

> In summing up the superiority of the Christian life over all other ways of living we cannot overlook the advantage that the Christian will have for all eternity. Job said, *"If a man dies, will he live again?"* (Job 14:14, NIV). He answered his own question when he said, *"For I know that my redeemer lives, And He shall stand at the last on the earth"* (Job 19:25).

> What a prospect! What a future! What a hope! What a life! ... to be a child of the King, a joint-heir with Christ, a member of the Royal Family of heaven!

> I know where I've come from, I know why I'm here, I know where I'm going—and I have peace in my heart. ...

Mr. Graham believed what his son preached.

Here on earth the influence of one who asks a favor for others depends upon his character; it is what he *is* that gives weight to what he *asks*. Just so, our power in prayer depends upon our life; where our life is right, we can please God. *"If you remain in me and my words remain in you, ask whatever you wish and it will be given you"* (John 15:7, NIV).

And, according to James, it is the "... *prayer of a righteous man*" that "*avails much*" (James 5:16).

We receive whatever we ask, John says, "... *because we keep His commandments.*" Obedience is involved, and this is "... *pleasing in His sight*" (1 John 3:22).

The life that can pray, and receive answers to those prayers, is the life that is abiding in Him; the life that, as a result, is pleasing God.

I had to learn these lessons as I matured in the Christian life. I did not always understand. Often I would wonder: What is it, Lord, that I am to be, or to do, that will enable me to pray as I should and receive what I ask? The answer came one day: One sentence, Morrow. It is the branch life.

The branch life? I reread John 15, the well-known parable of the vine and the branches. This was Jesus talking to His disciples. I knew the lesson He was conveying to them was of tremendous importance. We all know what a branch is—it is simply a growth of the vine, produced by it and appointed to bear fruit. Just as the vine only and wholly exists to produce the sap that makes the branch, so the branch has no other object but this alone—to receive that sap and bear the grapes. The relationship between Jesus and those who would be His true disciples in any age is like that of the vine and its branches. The believer is the branch of Christ, the heavenly vine;

therefore, we are to live so that Christ may bear fruit though us.

Instantly I saw it: With our life abiding in Him, and His words abiding in us, kept and obeyed in our hearts and lives, there would be grace to pray aright, and faith to receive whatsoever He wills.

I thought of men of old noted for their faith and faithfulness: Abraham, who forsook all for God; obedience was the law of his life. Moses, the intercessor; he too had forsaken all for God, *"Choosing rather to suffer affliction with the people of God, than to enjoy the passing pleasures of sin, esteeming the reproach of Christ greater riches than the treasures in Egypt. ..."* (Hebrews 11:25–26). Elijah, who stood up to plead for the Lord God of Israel. No wonder these men were bold in prayer; their hearts were right before God.

How well I knew that God longs to prove Himself the faithful God. Over and over again, in ever so many places, the Bible showed this to me. God had also proved this to me in His faithfulness to my own son and what He was accomplishing in Billy Frank's life.

Through the years, as individuals would ask me why there was so much seeming failure in their prayer-lives, I found myself pointing them to John 15 and sharing some of the lessons I'd learned.

We have not only Christ Himself, out of whose fullness and

grace we can draw, but we also have God the Father. Jesus said that He was the true vine, but His *"Father is the gardener"* (John 15:1, NIV). This means that the Father is watching over our abiding, our growth and fruit bearing.

"Every branch in Me that does not bear fruit He takes away; and every branch that bears fruit He prunes, that it may bear more fruit" (John 15:2). It is for fruit in our lives that the Husbandman cleanses the branches. Of all the fruit-bearing plants, there is none so ready to produce wild wood, and for which cleansing and pruning are so necessary, as the grape. What is it that the vinedresser cuts away with his pruning-knife? Wood—wild wood. Why cut away this wood? Because it draws away the strength and life from the vine, and hinders the flow of sap to the grape. The wood of the branch must decrease, that the fruit of the vine may increase. Even so, the child of God is a heavenly branch, and there is in us that which seems perfectly good and even legitimate, and yet draws out our interest and strength. It must be pruned, cleansed and cut away. How easy it is to let objects and cares of this world possess and overpower us.

I thought again about the power in prayer that men like Abraham, Moses and Elijah had (and the others mentioned in the roll-call-of-faith chapter—Hebrews 11). But the Bible plainly teaches what it cost them: God had to separate them from their surroundings, and draw them from any trust in themselves or others. The recognition came that it is only as our own strength, will and effort—even though they appear sinless and harmless—are cut down, taken out and removed from our lives, that we can bear real fruit for Him.

These were important lessons I learned about the life that can pray and experience answers to its praying. John 15:3 showed me what the pruning-knife is that the Father, the Husbandman, uses: "*You are already clean because of the word which I have spoken to you,*"(NIV). Later, in His high-priestly, intercessory prayer, Jesus lifted up His eyes to heaven and prayed: "*Sanctify them by Your truth: Your word is truth*" (John 17:17).

Through His Word the Father would cleanse the disciples, cut away all confidence in themselves (that is, in the flesh), and prepare them for the filling of the Spirit of the heavenly Vine. The lesson is so obvious for us—we cannot cleanse ourselves like that, God is the Husbandman.

Do we feel that we cannot live this branch life of abiding in Him? We are simply to trust Him to do in and through us what we cannot do for ourselves. I learned long ago that divine cleansing is usually a painful process. But God can be trusted to do the perfecting work of cleansing us to make us fruitful for Him—all that is unprofitable He will cut away—and as we trust and yield to Him, we find we can bear much fruit. The more simply we hold to this, and expect the Holy Spirit to do His share of the work, the more surely we will experience answers to our prayers.

Chapter Nine
Strangers and Pilgrims

Dear friends, I urge you, as aliens and strangers...
1 Peter 2:11, NIV

The believer is a pilgrim here upon earth. We are, as it were, just visitors passing through on our way to our heavenly destination. Those words, written by the Apostle Peter, have often helped me in my journey through life.

The idea expressed is that the condition of this world is such that we need to be reminded that we should allow nothing to impede our passage and our progress. We must not give in to the wickedness, temptations, problems and circumstances that arise to throw us off course. Our help comes in proportion to our recognition of this fact that life is a pilgrimage, but that God has left us much to guide and help us as pilgrims through this earthly scene.

As sojourners, strangers and exiles, we are to recognize

that we are actually engaged in combat—war is being made against our very souls. The conduct we should exhibit is laid out by Peter in the remaining verses in chapter two. Honorable, honest, righteous behavior should characterize our position as believers. Submission to those in authority, well doing, goodness, respect, love, kindness and consideration should be hallmarks identifying us as those who are following in Christ's footsteps.

Peter speaks of the suffering we will encounter too. His reminder is that Christ suffered, leaving us an example (see 1 Peter 2:21). God comforts the pilgrim—those who are cast down by circumstances. I have found it to be of great worth to be cast down, just to know such comfort as that! Think what it is to have God—a holy and righteous God—occupying Himself with us in our sorrows. When I remember who He is in my times of being cast down, then I am greatly encouraged. It is well to accept the complications of life as from God's hand. Let God keep the records. Peter says, *"Casting all your care upon Him; for He cares for you"* (1 Peter 5:7).

Peter is reminding us that this is God's personal invitation to cast the whole of our anxieties, worries, concerns—once and for all—on Him; for He cares for us affectionately, and He cares about us watchfully.

When the soul is cast down, like a ship when the tide is

low, it is in constant danger of shoals and sandbanks; but when the tide is up, there are no sandbanks, because the ship is lifted above them all. Just so, when heartaches come, if Christ is between us and the suffering, instead of the suffering getting between our hearts and Christ, then there follows a real blessing. *"No discipline seems pleasant at the time, but painful. Later on, however, it produces a harvest of righteousness and peace for those who have been trained by it"* (Hebrews 12:11, NIV).

We find ourselves afraid of consequences. However, as we walk day by day through faithfulness with the Lord, we should not fear consequences. We like to go along with a full, favorable south wind blowing, but a south wind does not always make for good sailing. It is more often the north winds that help us to grow in grace. The Apostle Paul would confirm that! He was beaten, stoned, shipwrecked. He knew weariness and pain; much bodily suffering. What did it do for Paul? There is sufficiency in Christ, Paul tells us:

> *... for I have learned in whatever state I am, to be content: I know how to be abased, and I know how to abound. Everywhere and in all things I have learned both to be full and to be hungry, both to abound and to suffer need. I can do all things through Christ who strengthens me.*
>
> Philippians 4:11–13

I can assure you, on the basis of a lifetime of sojourning and learning, that we experience more refreshment from the painful than from the pleasant things. It is astonishing what progress a soul makes in a time of sorrow and difficulty. The reason? There is much more confidence in God, more quietness and real dependence on Him; we feel our own weakness and helplessness. Through the trial, if our eyes are on Jesus, we can say like Him: "... *Shall I not drink the cup the Father has given me,*" (John 18:11, NIV). Every trial should become an occasion for perfecting obedience, otherwise it could become a temptation. Then, the Lord willing, it can be said of us when we come to journey's end: "*For we are to God the aroma of Christ...*" (2 Corinthians 2:15, NIV).

I've enjoyed my visit with you—this one-sided conversation— and I would hope you've been somewhat helped and encouraged. God in His great love understands and cares about you. Because He loved and cared so much, He has given us help and hope for now and the future—for all eternity. Along this pilgrimage pathway, He has left us with written instructions in His Word to us, the Bible. When we neglect this precious Word, we deprive ourselves of that which is so vital to spiritual growth and our total well-being. In it we are introduced to His Son, the Word who became flesh, the One who dwelt among us, full of life and love.

God has been good to us—the Graham family. Each one of us has experienced His hand of blessing and know His goodness. The world has seen and known my son Billy, and how God is using him. I often think of Psalm 73 where the psalmist says, "*Truly God is good to Israel, even to such as are of a clean heart*" (Psalms 73:1, KJV). I could insert there, "Truly God is good to Billy. ..."

In the Old Testament, Moses says, "*The Lord did not set His love on you nor choose you because you were more in number than any people. ... But because the Lord loves you*" (Deuteronomy 7:7, 8). I am sure people wonder and question why God should have chosen to use Billy in this way. I used to wonder about that myself; but then God directed me to these passages I have shared with you.

The only reason God can use any of us is because of His great love. *He loves because He loves*. He loves us all.

But God, who is rich in mercy, because of His great love with which He loved us, even when we were dead in trespasses, made us alive together with Christ (by grace you have been saved), and raised us up together, and made us sit together in the heavenly places in Christ Jesus, that in the ages to come He might show the exceeding riches of His grace in His kindness toward us in Christ Jesus. For by grace you have been saved through faith, and that not of yourselves; it is the gift of God, not of works, lest anyone should boast. For we are His workmanship, created in Christ Jesus for good works, which God prepared beforehand that we should walk in them.

Ephesians 2:4–10